Author Information

Lifted Spirits- A Manifestation Journal that will Change your Life by Leanne Evans

Leanne is a 31 year old transformational coach from South London. She always had a passion and gift for writing and creativity at a young age. This resulted in her achieving a BA Hons degree in English Literature and Film Studies. After graduating from De Montfort University, Leicester, Leanne embarked in a career in Marketing and PR she applied her energetic nature into climbing the corporate ladder.

Two tragic events including a bad breakup with her first love and the death of her father triggered Leanne to experience her spiritual awakening. She had realised that despite the outward projection of success she was not fulfilled or truly happy beneath the surface. She embarked on a quest for the truth.

Despite being bought us as a Catholic she had drifted away from her faith after leaving for University in Leicester. It was after these events however that Leanne began to seek something bigger than herself and to heal the areas of her life to lift her spirit. A family friend invited her to a local church. After years of seeking healing in New Age Practices and comfort in spiritualism she finally found self healing.

She realised it wasn't by performing, or living by strict religious dogma but rather by developing a relationship with God and receiving his love for the first time. She finally experienced true inner peace and a deep sense of freedom in all areas of her life.

Since developing this life changing relationship Leanne also began to experience miracles in her life. This included the healing of addictions, an end to self sabotaging behaviour, more intimacy, a healing of relationships and a higher self worth and purpose. Leanne now seeks to share the good news, all of the revelations she has experienced and her testimonies with the world to help others benefit as well.

She is passionate about supporting women to break through the bondage of not feeling worthy; of creating a life, and marketing the business of their wildest dreams. Her coaching services (1:1 & Group Coaching) and her Empowerment Facebook Community allows her the transformational space to lead women to experience the true liberty found in Christ. She wants to help others to reclaim Manifestation and its principles and anchor it to the word of God.

Dedication

I dedicate this book firstly to my spiritual dad, God, for being patient with me as I made my way back to you. To my earthly legendary Dad who believed in me even when I didn't believe in myself. To my incredible mum and sisters who have been my anchor throughout this crazy life. For the cats Bailey & Malibu for showing me how to love more every day. To all my beautiful friends, supporters and mentors I've had the pleasure to meet so far in life. To all the women out there who ever felt like they were not worthy of experiencing heaven on Earth. You are more worthy than you could imagine.

Prologue

The Lifted Spirits Manifestation Journal is here to support you on the journey of transforming your life. If you are unhappy with your life and do not know why, this journal will provide the answers.

We are all ultimately seeking happiness and fulfillment.

I have been blessed enough to have found the answer of how to achieve this. I was pleasantly surprised to realise that the path to happiness and prosperity was actually more simple than I ever could imagine. Since discovering this path my life has become a beautiful unfolding of miracles. I'm now sharing the secret of how you can experience miracles of your very own. The truth is you really can have it all. No matter what your life currently looks like. It can be done. You deserve to have all of the things that your heart desires and experience freedom, joy and expansion.

How is this manifestation journal different from others?

Lifted Spirits anchors the 7 manifestation principles in the power of God. It is a process of establishing a relationship with him, seeking his will for your life and surrendering to all of it.

Although this journal is written from my christian perspective I would like to stress that the precepts are applicable to any religion.

So grab your pen and let's complete the 7 simple steps to activate the power to achieve and receive all that you need in life.

The Lifted Spirits Manifestation Journal can be completed at your own pace. Each chapter is prefaced with a guiding scripture that you can meditate on and use to activate the power of the teachings in each chapter. Although the chapters are written in sequence, each chapter can be explored individually as well. Each chapter includes a brief teaching and an explorative exercise including journal prompts, visualizations to help you integrate the practices into your life. There are also reflective prompts and space available for you to explore in your own life what is revealed to you.

I want you to do what I have done in my life. Achieve happiness.

My spiritual journey

I have a tattoo on the back of my neck of a lotus flower which marks the start of me opening up to the spiritual realm. I always had a deep feeling that there was more to our life than what we could detect with our 5 senses. I began to explore the New Age practices of Yoga, Meditation and Manifestation alongside attending my local Christian Church. This opened me up to finally experiencing what I had always expected that we are more powerful than we could ever imagine. That we are capable of choice, growth, transformation and the ability to change our situations and circumstances or at least our perception of it.

I began to harness this power and transformed my self image from being anxious and shy to confident and outgoing. I manifested my dream job at the exact salary I had been writing about in my journal. My dream job as a life coach and countless holidays and fun experiences across the world were my reality. Behind the scenes of these incredible life experiences and seeming enjoyment of random events I was actually leading a very controlled life.

This included Scripting (A Manifestation Practice that involves writing in your journal as if you have already received the thing you wish to manifest), religiously seeking more and more knowledge every day, a pressure to do deep "shadow work" and to avoid spiritual bypassing (a practice where you confront your trauma and deepest fears and sit with the discomfort of bringing your shadow to the surface, rather than suppressing it)

This led to a lot of energy, time and focus centred on myself processing the world around me. I felt a sense of bondage to the practices and lifestyle of the New Age, an overwhelming fear that if I didn't keep us with New Moon Rituals and cleansing of negative energy, that I would not have the strength to maintain this new lifestyle I had built. New Moon Rituals involve a process of cleansing particular areas of your life to coincide with the phases of the moon cycle.

The lifestyle was extremely self righteous, I believed that my higher consciousness allowed me to live a better life.   By this point I was teaching women about all of the practices that have helped me to transform including the chakras, manifestation, yoga and the law of attraction. After the tragic death of George Floyd in May 2020 I experienced a racial awakening and felt the need to connect with my history and ancestors. I purchased the book <u>Sacred Woman: A Guide to Healing the Feminine Body, Mind, and Spirit</u> by Queen Afua.

The first chapter I read was around womb healing and involved a morning ritual, summoning the power of ancestors in the healing process. I never would have imagined that reading this book would have led to me experiencing my first encounter with God. Queen Afua does not follow Christian practices in fact she is a Spiritualist who promotes natural healing and ancestral wisdom as being key in the healing process. It was reading this book that led me to my first encounter with God.

I was in my local park, relaxing with my sister and began to experience extreme painful cramps in my womb area. I could barely walk and struggled to walk. It was at that moment when fear began to set in that I heard a voice. It said to me "everything you're doing in your business is demonic", there was no doubt in my mind at all that this was the voice of God. I had been seeking freedom from the confusion of the bondage, attachment and reliance I felt to the New Age world. There was no doubt in me at all that God was delivering me and giving me the clarity I had been seeking in the most bold overt way he could.

What resulted was a journey of me beginning to question the lifestyle I had created? If what I was doing was right, why did I feel so exhausted and depleted by striving to constantly improve. As I had always had a polygamous relationship with God and spirituality, I began to lean more of God rather than the New Age. It was at this point I began to truly transform for the better. I went from being completely self centred, spending all my money and time on me, trying to improve myself through courses and fulfilling my own ideas of my purpose to being liberated. I left behind the "situation-ships", the sabotaging behaviors, the pressure of playing God in my life to letting the real God and creator take over.

My life has transformed in so many ways from that point. I'm healthier, happier, more fulfilled and more inspired than I could ever imagine possible. I feel a sense of freedom everyday; freedom to express myself, to receive love and to give this love to others. I now no longer practice any New Age practices in my life. I fully worship God. With my testimony I am not here to condemn anyone. The only one who can judge us is God, I am just here to share my lived experience and the breakthroughs I've had. This manifestation journal is for all God seekers, whatever your religion is.

"All things are yours"

I Corinthians 3:21-23

What would make you feel truly fulfilled in life?

For me, fulfillment came when I realised my purpose in life. Not the purpose society dictated to me, but my God given purpose. I was able to express myself as his unique creation and use my gifts to positively impact the lives of others around me. A revelation occured for me when I realised that true fulfillment comes from thinking of others and sharing God's unconditional love with them as much as this can. This can be a struggle at times! I also experienced fulfillment realising that I don't have to be perfect, that it is ok to make mistakes. Life is a journey and I don't have to be so impatient to reach an undefined destination.

Do you truly believe that you can attain this?

I didn't believe that I could attain what I wanted in life. I had a lot of brokenness within me; heartbreak, trauma, repressed pain, guilt and shame. This all limited my perception of my life and what was possible for me. Through my healing journey I have been able to realise my true power and feel worthy to attain all I wanted. To manifest power fully we need to activate our faith, in God and in ourselves. Once I began the journey of activating my faith and trust I was able to achieve freedom. I have since been able to rebuild my relationships, build two thriving businesses and feel on fire in my life!

What do you truly believe that you can attain in your life?

What would you like to attain in your life?

Journal Time

_____
_____
_____
_____
_____
_____
_____
_____
_____
_____
_____
_____
_____
_____
_____
_____
_____
_____

_____

_____

_____

_____

_____

_____

_____

_____

_____

_____

_____

_____

_____

_____

_____

_____

_____

_____

_____

_____

This journal is here to show you that you can be anchored by the promises of God. In my own journey I have been blessed to see the miracles of God again and again. He has never let me down.

Through his love and grace I have gone from drink dependency, low self esteem, shame,seeking external validation and being disconnected from love to falling in love with myself and creating a life of abundance. I now know that anything is possible. It is possible for you.

What is it that you think you need to improve? Don't worry we are going to work through this together. Take a moment now to reflect and review the areas of life you want to improve and bring more abundance into

Journal Time

_____

_____

_____

_____

_____

_____

_____

_____

_____

_____

_____

_____

_____

This journal seeks to guide you through the 7 step process to manifesting a life of your wildest dreams using the power of our creator. This will not only help you get clarity on what you want to manifest but also begin the transformation process of allowing you to see yourself as the incredible gift worthy of every blessing in life.

God has blessed me personally in so many ways, even up to the completion of this book God has connected me with the right people at just the right time. I met with no less than 3 people in one week, who had self published a book and an editor who was happy to help me refine this journal and show me how to do the whole process. This is only one example of how the creator has supported me.

What examples have you experienced of God's blessings?

Journal Time

_____

_____

_____

_____

_____

_____

_____

_____

_____

_____

_____

_____

_____

_____

Abundance has always struck me as being such a beautiful word. This is what I believe every woman deserves; to be living a life which is overflowing in love, joy, peace and fulfilment. True freedom from the bondage of this world is by not playing small. If you don't believe you are worthy of having the things you want in life you wont get them. By following the steps in this journey you will begin to receive all of the incredible things that God has waiting for you. Most importantly you will develop a strong relationship with him and trust him as the true creator of your life.

For me everything changed when I stopped listening to the world and it's cultural view of my identity and instead started to learn about God's vision for my creation. As a black woman there are so many elements of society that prohibit us from experiencing our greatness. When I started to explore the word, I found a new narrative that started to challenge some of the implicit racism and conditioning I experienced. Instead of being stereotyped and isolated I was told that "God created man in His *own* image; in the image of God. He created him; male and female He created them" When I started to focus my energy into learning these truths from the bible I began an incredible process of being transformed, empowered by discovering the real me. Worthiness and self love anchored in who we really are is the key to living a fulfilling life. When I took this step to move past being the anxious, people-pleasing girl seeking validation and love in any way she can, I became an empowered woman. The results of this were astounding. Fake friends fell away, I stopped allowing myself to be used, I started to respect my body and mind in such a more profound way. I had all of this positive energy to put into creating a life of my wildest dreams.

Happy Manifesting Beautiful Souls

Leanne

"For I am persuaded that neither death nor life, nor angels nor principalities nor powers, nor things present nor things to come, nor height nor depth, nor any other created thing, shall be able to separate us from the love of God which is in Christ Jesus our Lord."
Romans 8:38-39

1.   Getting Closer to God

One of the things that separates the Lifted Spirits Manifestation process from those rooted in New Age Principles is that New Ageism is a movement which seeks alternative approaches to traditional Western culture, with an interest in spirituality, mysticism, holism, and environmentalism. With New Age Manifestation the focus is on manifesting the things that we want, and us ultimately taking the role of God. With the Lifted Spirit method instead we surrender to the will of God. Can we say that we truly know that these things will make us happy? The secret to living a life of your wildest dreams is aligning with God's vision for you. His vision holds the secret for your most expansive, fulfilling and transformational journey. So the key is to develop your relationship with him so he can begin to share with you the path to your most incredible life. However if developing a good relationship with God was that easy then there would be no reason for this journal. God is often whispering in our ear and guiding us but are we open and still enough to hear him? We have so many other focuses in our life from our jobs, businesses and social calendar. Are you really allowing space to connect with God in your life? To start seeing manifestation miracles, we need to put God at the top of our priority list. Not just to get the things we want out of life, but to build a relationship with him so we can become a co-creator for his plans for us.

What are the hallmarks of the most fruitful relationships you have?

Journal Time

_____

_____

_____

_____

_____

_____

_____

_____

_____

_____

_____

_____

_____

_____

_____

_____

_____

For me it is the ability to be able to speak about anything without shame, to be able to rely on that person, to trust that person, to be able to experience joy and feel good around them. What do I give back to the relationship? I listen, I give my time, I make space in all areas of my life to accommodate this person and to try and make them happy. This is exactly the type of reciprocal relationship that we want to try and create with God.

I've always been a seeker of love, this has sadly led to countless unrequited experiences in my life! I remember I used to be so fixated on my crush at the time, constantly thinking of them, anticipating and doing all I could to impress them and make them happy. It is this level of fascination and hunger we need to have in wanting to love God more. We are told to "seek first the kingdom of God and His righteousness, and all these things shall be added to you" Matthew 6:33 "These things" are all of the earthly things that we are conditioned to desire and seek daily.

The first step of the Lifted Spirits Manifestation process is so powerful as we are told, when we seek God first, all of the other areas we wish to manifest will come into our life with very little effort.

Your first manifestation exercise is to practice with 4 powerful questions to help you really connect with God.

You will become aware of your current blockers to connect with him, how you currently connect and your aspirations of how you want your relationship to flourish by the end of this journey.

I advise completing these journal questions in a quiet undisturbed area of your home where you feel comfortable and relaxed. Take a moment to slow down before you begin and allow yourself the space to not rush and see what unfolds.

Exercise 1

Journal Prompts

1. What needs to change in your life so you can become closer with God?

2. How can you connect more with God on a daily basis and how can you implement this?

3. How do you currently see God's presence in your life? Eg a father figure, a friend, a guide?

4. How would you like your relationship to be with God at the end of this journey?

Journal Time

_____
_____
_____
_____
_____
_____
_____
_____
_____

"Where there is no revelation, the people cast off restraint; But happy is he who keeps the law."
Proverbs 29:18

2.   God Given Vision

Whatever you focus on will magnify in your life. So it is important that we elevate our vision of our life to God's standard. As you begin to draw closer to God just like a friend he will begin to make his secrets and vision clearer to you. At this point it is pivotal that you pay close attention to your experience with life. Are you finding changes occurring? Wanting to spend your time, energy and focus on doing different things? Getting new ideas and a fire in your heart to explore new things? These are all signs that the Holy Spirit is guiding you into the new vision of your life.

When we have no vision in our lives we get swept up in fulfilling somebody else's expectations. For years I had no God-given vision. I was hustling in the rat race of life. Life seemed to have a very narrow and defined structure. Do well at school, get the degree, work your way up to the highest salary possible, get a mortgage, hopefully a husband, have a family, retire somewhere nice, enjoy my pension then die.

As I drew closer to God however, he began to reveal to me his God given vision which was vastly different from this rigid plan. Six years ago I started to write down the insights I was getting about God's given vision for me (The image shown below is the actual page written six years ago). This included becoming a coach, having a successful wellbeing business, supporting and empowering women with feeling worthy, blogging and publishing a bestselling book. At the time of writing these revelations from God I was taking part in a CBT (Cognitive Behaviour Therapy) course to support me with my high levels of anxiety, I was binge drinking every weekend and having casual sex with people I barely knew.

I think you can see for yourself how vastly different God's vision was compared to my own for myself at the time. But as I started to become clearer on God's given vision for me, what my heart desired began to change. How was I going to achieve everything he had shown me by continuing living my life in this way. I began to make small changes, becoming more aware about my drinking habits, questioning what I was truly seeking from my sexual encounters. My awareness and curiosity continued to develop, and I allowed the healing of drawing closer to God to help me grow.

It has been a messy journey, which is still continuing now but I am happy to say I have manifested God's Vision that I wrote down all of those years ago. Still waiting on receiving the OBE (Order of the British Empire). This is an honour bestowed by the Queen of England. The beautiful thing is that the vision is never complete so we have a lifetime of manifesting God's glory and making his vision our reality.

Career

Breakthrough Goal
- Receive an OBE.

Be a Millionaire
Have this amount in the bank by 08/10/20

Have a successful Health + Wellbeing empire (ReBubble)

Retreats in carribean + Africa teaching self esteem

Blog about health, wellbeing + beauty

Health coaching private clients + corporate companies

Have a bestselling book under the ReBubble Brand

Visualisation Exercise

Take some time in a quiet place where you will be undisturbed to lie down. Use your imagination to visualize how you can begin to improve the areas of your life.

Once you've had some time to visualize the individual areas, take some time to write about what vision God placed in your heart for each.

Once you have completed your record, select the area of your life that you would like to focus on in terms of manifesting for the next month. Pick one task that you want to focus on for each month. This will make the process easier. It will be easier to see the results of your manifestations.

Finances

Journal Time

_____
_____
_____
_____
_____
_____
_____
_____
_____
_____
_____
_____
_____
_____
_____
_____
_____
_____
_____
_____
_____
_____
_____

Relationships

Journal Time

_____

_____

_____

_____

_____

_____

_____

_____

_____

_____

_____

_____

_____

_____

_____

_____

_____

_____

_____

_____

_____

_____

_____

Spirituality

Journal Time

_____
_____
_____
_____
_____
_____
_____
_____
_____
_____
_____
_____
_____
_____
_____
_____
_____
_____
_____
_____
_____
_____
_____
_____
_____
_____
_____
_____
_____

Health

Journal Time

_____
_____
_____
_____
_____
_____
_____
_____
_____
_____
_____
_____
_____
_____
_____
_____
_____
_____
_____
_____
_____
_____
_____
_____
_____

Fitness

Journal Time

_____
_____
_____
_____
_____
_____
_____
_____
_____
_____
_____
_____
_____
_____
_____
_____
_____
_____
_____
_____
_____
_____
_____

Home Environment

Journal Time

_____

_____

_____

_____

_____

_____

_____

_____

_____

_____

_____

_____

_____

_____

_____

_____

_____

_____

_____

_____

_____

_____

_____

_____

_____

Career

Journal Time

_____

_____

_____

_____

_____

_____

_____

_____

_____

_____

_____

_____

_____

_____

_____

_____

_____

_____

_____

_____

_____

_____

_____

_____

Social Life

Journal Time

_____
_____
_____
_____
_____
_____
_____
_____
_____
_____
_____
_____
_____
_____
_____
_____
_____
_____
_____
_____
_____
_____
_____

Joy

Journal Time

_____
_____
_____
_____
_____
_____
_____
_____
_____
_____
_____
_____
_____
_____
_____
_____
_____
_____
_____
_____
_____
_____
_____
_____
_____

Creativity

Journal Time

_____
_____
_____
_____
_____
_____
_____
_____
_____
_____
_____
_____
_____
_____
_____
_____
_____
_____
_____
_____

"Be anxious for nothing, but in everything by prayer and supplication, with thanksgiving, let your requests be made known to God; and the peace of God, which surpasses all understanding, will guard your hearts and minds through Christ Jesus."
Philippians 4:6-7

3.   Prayer & Gratitude

We have nothing to be anxious about as we have the most powerful tool to manifest. This is prayer. The word of God holds all of his promises for us, his word tells us when we pray in a state of thanksgiving for all that we already have, we will experience a divine peace which will place us in the "frequency" to be able to receive all of our blessings.

We need to posture ourselves to thank God as if we have already received the things that we are trying to manifest. Are you waiting for your soul mate partner or that new business to flourish? When you pray, thank God, acting as if you have the thing you are asking for already. E.g "Thank you so much for bringing my soulmate into my life. He has brought so much joy and excitement, I am becoming a better woman from even being in his presence, I'm so thankful to have met him".

When we pray we open up a powerful portal to connect directly with the one who created us and who is truly our source for everything. In New Age practices we are told to ask the universe and it will be given.   But with this Manifestation Guide we instead speak, acknowledge and respect God. For me my manifesting journey gained momentum when I took my prayer life seriously.

The truth is that we have access to a prayer room at all times in our heart. We can get into a habit where we can begin to speak the true longings to God from our heart which he will always hear and make happen. Things are taken to another level when we consciously make a specific time to pray and in a way that allows for reverence and gratitude to God. I now schedule this sacred time at the end of the day.

Once I have completed my day, have my pyjamas and am ready to snuggle up in bed, I kneel at my altar and begin my sacred prayer time. I invite the Holy Spirit to commune with me and I begin then to speak authentically. If you can't kneel there is of course the option to pick what feels comfortable for you.

I always thank God for the doors he has opened and those we have shut. As you continue this process you will begin to see that even when things look negative from our perception. We begin to lean on God in these times and trust that he will find a resolution better than we could even imagine in his timing.

One of the most incredible parts of starting this ritual of prayer and gratitude has been seeing the results. I advise writing down your prayers so you can keep track. I have witnessed my prayers for others manifesting before my eyes; from healings, people being offered new homes to live in and new incredible opportunities. There really is no end to God's miraculous power when it comes from prayer.

How have you seen the miracle of prayer work in your own life?

Write a prayer to God around the area of your life that you wish to focus on in terms of manifesting over the next month

Journal Prompts

_____
_____
_____
_____
_____

Exercise- Create a Prayer Altar

Find a quiet undisturbed part of your home. Get a small table and place meaningful objects on there such as your bible (or a book relating to your faith) candles, perhaps an image of the God you worship etc. (Place a comfortable cushion in front of the table that you can kneel (if you cannot kneel you can sit) on for prayer.

Spend time in the morning before you start your day and in the evening before prayer at your space for prayer. See this as a beautiful, sacred time where you can connect with God and speak all of the desires of your heart, even if he knows them already!

"Therefore I urge you, brothers and sisters, by the mercies of God, to present your bodies [dedicating all of yourselves, set apart] as a living sacrifice, holy and well-pleasing to God, which is your rational (logical, intelligent) act of worship."
Romans 12:1

4.   Purifying our Life

We live in a world that is plagued by so much darkness. Sickness, death, pain, grief is all part of our human experience. Satan is the ruler of this world and his primary aim is to "steal, and to kill, and to destroy" John 10:10.

In order to receive our blessings we have to believe that we are worthy of them. When we get to a place where we feel worthy we are able to close the doors to the things that are keeping us stagnant and caught up in unhealthy cycles. What is on the other side of closing these doors; the fruits of walking in the spirit, joy, love, peace and freedom from bondage.

For me in my journey the biggest obstacle I've had to overcome was negative self-talk spurred on from a feeling of unworthiness. Now I look back and see that I was plagued by a constant cycle of lies. We all have that negative voice that can creep in. The voice that tells you that nobody wants to hear what you have to say. The voice that tells you that you are unlovable or keeps replaying negative things from your past in your mind. This is not the voice of God.

As you immerse yourself in this manifestation process you will become empowered to be aware of this negative voice; challenge and silence it. For me on my purification journey I had to break free of the things that I noticed increased this negative, restrictive thought process. This included excessive drinking and being around fake friends so I could become the most authentic version of myself. I'm not saying I never have negative thoughts, but I am saying that I have more discernment and authority about which thoughts I let dictate my life.

What are you allowing and enabling in your life that is stopping you from elevating yourself to receive all of the blessings that are owed to you?

How is your joy in life currently being compromised?

Journal Time

_____
_____
_____
_____
_____
_____

Exercise

Fasting & Purify Me- Journal Confession

Fasting is such a beautiful spiritual practice to help you feel more intimate and connected to God as well as purifying yourself from all of the distractions of this world. At various points of the bible we see it used as a discipline to connect directly with God to receive revelation. This is a spiritual practice adopted by many religions. I am going to guide you through the simple fasting practice that I use.

Fasting, as beautiful as it is, is one of the hardest spiritual practices for me. But it is for this reason that it actually has such powerful results. God sees us making a sacrifice and will reward us for this. Always use your discernment when it comes to fasting. If the time frames don't work for you, you're on medication, or just really can't imagine not eating for hours, always be honest with yourself if this is the best time for you to commit to your fast. We don't want to do fasting as a performative exercise to feel validated rather we want to cut off from our attachments and lean in and surrender to our source God, supporting us. We are giving our body as a living sacrifice and showing God that we are serious about discovering his will and manifesting it.

Perhaps fasting is something that can assist you with the area you wish to focus on in regards to manifesting over the next month. So why not fast to overcome unhealthy habits, overspending, giving your energy to things which do not elevate you? Why not allow God to give you the strength to overcome what may be preventing you from manifesting the thing you want? We do not need to rely on our own strength and can use fasting to provide us the inner power to overcome any barriers.

Esther 3 Day Intermittent Fast Esther is a prominent Jewish woman in the bible who ultimately led her people to victory. In order to build up her confidence and strength, Esther asked the Jewish people to fast for three days and nights on her behalf before she went on to plead for the mercy of her people. These three days of fasting were a national rallying cry for salvation. The whole nation was united behind Esther, and God indeed answered their prayers. "Go, gather all the Jews who are present in Shushan, and fast for me; neither eat nor drink for three days, night or day. My maids and I will fast likewise. And so I will go to the king, which *is* against the law; and if I perish, I perish!"

Esther's story is an incredible revelation of the power that fasting can bring us. Esther had a clear idea of the outcome she wanted to manifest and used fasting as a means for God to step in and use his power to free her people.

You can pick to fast from sunrise to midday, 3pm or 6pm- I usually do until 3 pm.

There are many types of fasts, and the option you choose depends upon your health, the desired length of your fast, and your preference: • A Water Fast - means to abstain from all food and juices • A Partial Fast - means to eliminate certain foods or specific meals • A "Juice" Fast - means to drink only fruit or vegetable juices during meal times. I know the prospect of going without food for an extended period of time may be of concern to some. But there are ways to ensure that your body is getting the nutrients it needs, so you can remain safe and healthy during your fast.

I usually only consume liquids within my selected timeframes. This is usually water and occasionally tea for me. I tend to stay away from coffee while I'm fasting as it is a stimulant.

The important thing to remember while you fast is to focus on God. We are supposed to spend the time we would have spent preparing a meal or being distracted to connect with the word and to pray directly to God about anything that is revealed to us.

I have listed some incredible resources at the end of this journal if you wish to find out more about fasting and if it is an option you would like to support you as you complete this chapter.

Exercise- Purify Me
Journal Confession

This is time for you to get truly honest with yourself about the areas you want to purify in your life. These are the things that fill your time on the surface but when you dig deeper you realise that they are bringing no true fulfillment or value to your life. This could include gossiping, casual sex, excessive drinking and drugs; seeking power and knowledge, seeking external validation.

If you are choosing to fast please complete the prompts on Day 3 of your fast. If you're not fasting you can complete this exercise when you are ready as you go through this chapter.

Write and complete the following

Dear God, I am surrendering and choosing to allow your power to work through me, rather than trying to do things on my own strength. I know that I need to purify my life and say goodbye to… (For me this meant saying goodbye to seeking external validation, people pleasing and being fearful of expressing the authentic version of me)

Journal Time

_____
_____
_____
_____
_____
_____
_____
_____
_____
_____
_____
_____
_____
_____
_____
_____
_____
_____
_____
_____
_____
_____
_____
_____
_____
_____
_____

_____

_____

_____

_____

_____

_____

_____

_____

_____

_____

_____

_____

_____

_____

_____

_____

_____

_____

_____

God I know that in order to allow your glory to shine through me; I do not need to walk this journey alone and that you have sent a companion in the Holy Spirit to raise me up and set me apart in this world. Please allow me to see myself as you see me and to show my purity as a gift in this world.

For the word of God is living and powerful, and sharper than any two-edged sword, piercing even to the division of soul and spirit, and of joints and marrow, and is a discerner of the thoughts and intents of the heart. Hebrews 4:12

"Therefore I say to you, whatever things you ask when you pray, believe that you receive them, and you will have them. Mark 11:24

5.   Raising our Faith Levels- Speaking words over your life

Part of the magic of manifesting is raising your faith levels to believe you can receive anything that you ask for. We are told that all of the promises in the bible are living and powerful. This means that when we declare these promises over our life we are certain to see them manifest in our future. This is an opportunity for you to get bold and stand in our power as children of God harnessing the power he has given you to make some incredible changes in your life. When we declare these affirmations to ourselves it helps to renew us, build our spirit and increase our hope and faith.

The currency of heaven is said to be faith. To have faith is in fact a spiritual gift. I have always been blessed to possess an incredible amount of faith in my life. This has been especially apparent at times when I have had every reason to crumble. In 2019 I was busy working at Treatwell, the beauty booking app. As a Commercial Manager I was responsible for managing all of the salons in West London.

My days consisted of face to face meetings and the occasional freebie if I was lucky. I had recently moved back home after living with a friend. I noticed my dad had lost a bit of weight and seemed to be more tired and reserved than usual but I didn't put too much thought into it. I was on a day of back to back meetings as usual in Fulham.

My dad had gone into hospital after a few weeks of being more tired than usual. I had just arrived at my meeting, which was in a nail bar on the high street. As I got ready to get my laptop out I noticed several missed calls from my mum. I excused myself and called straight back. She answered with a sombre tone and told me to come straight to the hospital.

As soon as I hung the phone up my world completely changed forever, I felt sick, I stumbled around and felt tears falling over my face. I excused myself and rushed to the hospital. My dad was diagnosed with stage 4 stomach cancer that afternoon. He died 2 weeks later. There is no experience quite like losing a loved one. I felt raw, exposed, lower than low. For the first time in my life my faith was completely gone. I felt hopeless and couldn't imagine life ever being worth living again.

God is not only there for the high moments when we are manifesting and feeling good, it is at these low points that we need him more than ever to help heal our hearts. I was patient with myself while trying to rebuild myself. I had a strong awareness that I could never go back to who I was before but I acknowledged this was an opportunity to begin to activate my faith again; to become the person I know my dad could be proud of. Whilst being confronted by God I began to start to write and declare the woman I wanted to become.

I used the exercise you are going to complete to rebuild myself. Faith is a powerful tool and in this moment in my life I realised just how powerful. I stopped drinking completely for a year, moved to a new job in the industry I wanted with a 15 k salary increase but most importantly I found my faith again.

Exercise- Your Declarations

Here are 10 declarations anchored in the word that you can begin to start speaking over your life. Feel free edit or add to this list based on the things you want to manifest in your life and your area of focus for the month

1 – I DECLARE an explosion of God's incredible blessings over my life. I will see a sudden demonstration of God's goodness and increase in all areas of my life

2 – I DECLARE I will experience God's faithfulness. I refuse to worry or doubt. I will keep my trust in Him, knowing that He will never fail me.

3 – I DECLARE that today I am motivated, full of power, strength, and determination. Nothing I face will be too much for me. I will overcome every obstacle, outlast every challenge, and come through every difficulty better off than I was before.

4 – I DECLARE it is not too late to accomplish everything God has placed in my heart. I have not missed my purpose or window of opportunity. God is about to accelerate me to help me accomplish

that dream. This is my time. This is my moment. I will receive it today!

5 – I DECLARE I am grateful for who God is in my life and for what he has done. I will not take for granted the people, the opportunities, and the favor he has blessed me with. I will find the positives rather than what is wrong.

6 – I DECLARE that God is bringing about a new season of growth in my life. I will not get stagnant and hold on to the old. I will be open to change knowing that God has something better in front of me. New doors of opportunity, new relationships, and new levels of joy and excitement are in my future.

7 – I DECLARE that God has a great plan for my life. He is directing my steps. And even though I may not always understand how, I know my situation is always working out for my highest good. God will work it out in his perfect timing.

8– I DECLARE God's dream for my life is coming to pass. It will not be stopped by people, disappointments, or adversities. God has solutions to every problem I will ever face already lined up.

The right people and the right breaks are in my future. I will fulfill my destiny. This is my declaration. 9– I DECLARE I will pair action with my faith. I will not be passive or indifferent. I will demonstrate my faith by taking bold steps to move toward what God has put in my heart. My faith will not be hidden; it will be seen.

10 – I DECLARE that I am calm and peaceful. I will not let people or circumstances upset me, there is an anointing of true ease to my life. I will rise above every difficulty, knowing that God has given me the power to remain calm.

What areas do you want to activate more faith into your life?

Journal Time

_____
_____
_____
_____
_____
_____
_____
_____
_____
_____
_____
_____
_____
_____
_____
_____
_____
_____
_____
_____
_____
_____
_____

"Therefore submit to God. Resist the devil and he will flee from you."
James 4:7

6.   Surrendering

I used to view surrender as a weak word. The thought of letting go of control and giving up my power as a woman felt counter intuitive to all of the incredible transitions we have made in history. But when we surrender to God we dont lose anything we only gain.

The truth is we don't have as much control as we may think, we only need to look at what has transpired over the last couple of years to realise this. We take on average 20,000 breaths per day, and God is responsible for every single one. Do you want to continue toiling to work out what your next move should be?

Should you invest in that programme?

Should you take that new job?

Should you continue in a relationship that isn't fulfilling you or adding value to your life?

Rather than worrying and trying to figure things out when you can never truly know the right answer, how about collaborating with God? When we surrender we allow the Holy Spirit to flow within us and begin to work miracles.

This was one of the most challenging parts of the manifestation process for me. I always thought I had fully surrendered to God and was able to do so in so many areas of my life but the one sticky area has always been my business. But there was still a degree of me wanting to do things in the way I thought was best. Or I would say yes to opportunities that would arise without seeking his guidance or truly contemplating if this was part of my God Given vision. When this happened I ended up delaying receiving my own blessings. Trying to do things my way resulted in life lessons but did not activate my highest purpose.

Sometimes when we continue to do things in our own way, God has to really teach us that we don't always know best. This was the case for me earlier in the year in my business. My spirit was telling me to rest, I was feeling burnt out and mentally and physically exhausted. But having just completed a sales training which showed a marketing technique to help grow your coaching business, I felt compelled to give the method a try in my own business. The model comprised several different components each one more energetically consuming then the last, from lead generation on social media, to delivering a whole week long virtual retreat.

I prided myself as I followed each part of the method flawlessly, I had an incredible sign up rate and was so excited to deliver the retreat and to gain some new clients. Day 1 came and despite 100 sign ups only 4 faces were looking back at me on zoom.

I decided to not let this bring me down and continued with the week. One day, there were no attendees at all. Despite flawlessly following the formula I received no new clients at the end. Exhausted, disappointed and at the end of my tether trying to do things my way, at the end of the process, I finally surrendered my business to God. I got on my knees and completely gave control to him to show me what I should do next.

The truth is although I was flawlessly following the formula, this was not God's formula. Since surrendering I have been able to step into the role of co-creator. I finally rested, allowed parts of me to be healed and surrendered to the vision of God.

The results have been this journal you're completing now!

Exercise- I Surrender Visualization Exercise

Imagine floating on a giant cloud, in a dazzling pink sky. You are secure on this cloud as it safely guides you across the beautiful sky. As part of your incredible journey you are able to drop into the sky surrounding you with all of the things which you are currently thinking about and trying to change. These are the areas of your life that you're now choosing to surrender to God. You can surrender your love, life, your career, your health etc to God. Acknowledge how you feel after you drop each area.

After you drop your area's into the sky say this short prayer

Dear God, thank you for walking this journey of life with me and for all that you have blessed me with good and what I perceived as bad. I know that I cannot control everything in my life and I no longer wish to. I want to collaborate with you instead of trying to manifest on my own strength. From this point on I surrender

Journal Time

I put my life in your hands. I will now no longer be anxious. Instead I will use the armour of prayer and faith to trust that all will be done in your wisdom. I am excited to see the demonstration of this surrender in my life and know that the manifestation will be above and beyond anything I can imagine

"Teacher, which is the great commandment in the law?" Jesus said to him, "'You shall love the Lord your God with all your heart, with all your soul, and with all your mind.' This is the first and great commandment.

And the second is like it: 'You shall love your neighbor as yourself.' On these two commandments hang all the Law and the Prophets."
Matthew 22:36-40

7.Serving Others

With manifestation often we are seeking ultimate fulfillment in our lives. Our God is a God of love. Jesus has taught which are the most important commandments that he guides us to live by. One of these is to love our neighbour as we love ourselves. So what if we were to consider others with the things that we are looking to manifest in our lives? When we pour our love into others we experience heaven on this earth and truly embody our divine purpose of being divine vessels of love.

Our society has forced us into becoming extremely self centred, becoming ruthless in our pursuit of the best paid job, buying our home and keeping our lives busy. We lose sight of the ultimate aim of our existence. To love our creator, receive that love and use it to love ourselves and then to share this love out to others.

For me now there is no greater experience than giving love to others and serving them in any way I can. This doesn't have to be just the big things. Giving someone a smile, telling someone close to you something you love about them or prioritising others before yourself can be one of the most fulfilling things you could do today. I have never been so self centred as when I was practicing New Ageism. I was so focused on my healing journey, of reaching this stage of enlightenment and keeping my vibration high that I was unable to be grounded, present and to connect with those around me that I love.

One of the most refreshing things about the Lifted Spirits Manifestation process is that we factor others into our lives. Relationships are key to existence, fulfillment and happiness. God had to create Eve as a companion and somebody to reflect love back to Adam. It is the same for us. We can have all of the material possessions you could think of but if there is nobody to share this with, to witness our breakthroughs and celebrate our journey is it really as sweet?

Yes, it's ok to want that new car, but how can this car also support others in your life? Yes you would like more money in your account, but will this extra income allow you to give to others or to grow your ability to support others.

If loving others was so easy, we wouldn't find it such a struggle day to day. Here are some journal prompts to help you identify what blockers could be preventing you from giving love more freely to those in your life

Journal Questions

1.   How would you describe the energy of your heart right now?

Journal Time

_____
_____
_____
_____
_____
_____
_____
_____
_____
_____
_____
_____
_____
_____
_____
_____
_____
_____
_____
_____

2.   In what ways do you feel that love for others is absent in your life?

Journal Time

_____
_____
_____
_____
_____
_____
_____
_____
_____
_____
_____
_____
_____
_____
_____
_____
_____
_____
_____
_____
_____

3. What is one step you can take today to be more loving to others in your life?

Journal Time

_____
_____
_____
_____
_____
_____
_____
_____
_____
_____
_____
_____
_____
_____
_____
_____
_____
_____
_____
_____
_____

4.   In what ways can you move from a self centred mindset and let love flow more freely to others?

Journal Time

_____
_____
_____
_____
_____
_____
_____
_____
_____
_____
_____
_____
_____
_____
_____
_____
_____
_____

You have now completed all 7 steps of the Lifted Spirits Manifestation Journal! Thank you for walking the journey with an open mind and heart. I trust you are now ready to be bold, move in miracles and start to enjoy all of the blessings you have been manifesting.

Love Always

Leanne xx

Contact
Instagram-
https://instagram.com/leanneevanswellbeing?igshid=lwhfabgrfmai
Email-hello@leannevanswellbeing.com
Website-https://www.leanneevanswellbeing.com/

Additional Resources

Fasting
https://www.healthyhildegard.com/spiritual-fasting/

https://www.cru.org/us/en/train-and-grow/spiritual-growth/fasting/7-steps-to-fasting.2.html

Printed in Great Britain
by Amazon

74873642R00078